OFFICIAL DISCARD
LaGrange County Public Library

LAGRANGE COUNTY LIBRARY
BOOKMOBILE

Y0-CUP-501

j796.323
DE

DE MEDEIROS, MICHAEL
NATIONAL BASKETBALL
ASSOCIATION FINALS

Scribbles on back page 10-15-24 CT

CHAMPIONSHIPS

NBA FINALS

Michael De Medeiros

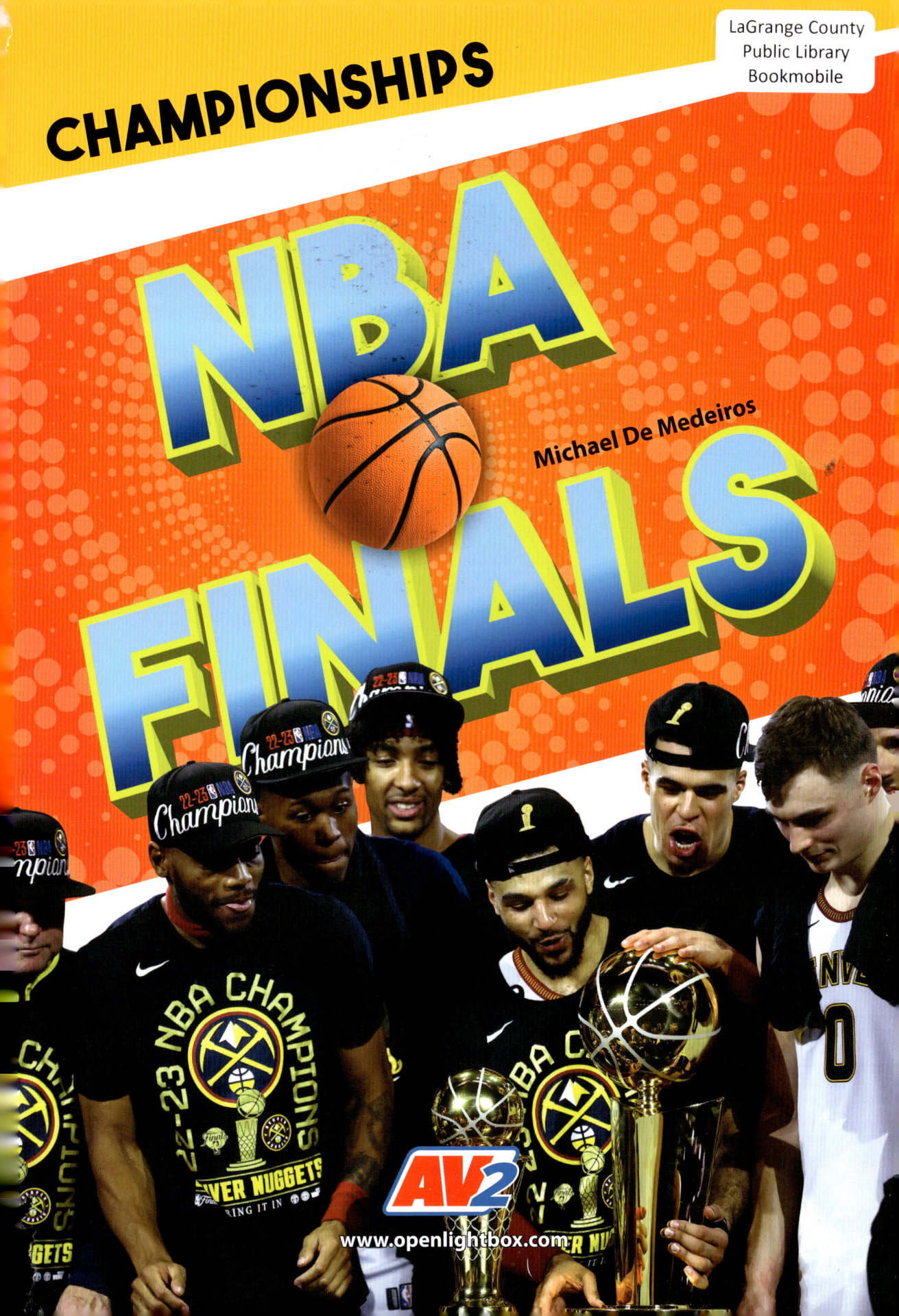

LaGrange County Public Library Bookmobile

AV2

www.openlightbox.com

AV2

Step 1
Go to www.openlightbox.com

Step 2
Enter this unique code

LXBQUB2TJ

Step 3
Explore your interactive eBook!

CONTENTS
- 4 What Is the NBA Finals?
- 6 The History
- 8 The Rules
- 10 The Basketball Court
- 12 Players on the Team
- 13 The Equipment
- 14 Qualifying to Play
- 16 The Main Event
- 18 Where They Play
- 20 Women in Basketball
- 22 Important Moments
- 24 Legends and Current Stars
- 26 All-Time Records
- 28 NBA Finals Timeline
- 30 Test Your Knowledge

AV2 is optimized for use on any device

Your interactive eBook comes with...

Contents
Browse a live contents page to easily navigate through resources

Audio
Listen to sections of the book read aloud

Videos
Watch informative video clips

Weblinks
Gain additional information for research

Slideshows
View images and captions

Try This!
Complete activities and hands-on experiments

Key Words
Study vocabulary, and complete a matching word activity

Quizzes
Test your knowledge

Share
Share titles within your Learning Management System (LMS) or Library Circulation System

Citation
Create bibliographical references following APA, CMOS, and MLA styles

This title is part of our AV2 digital subscription

1-Year Grades K–5 Subscription
ISBN 978-1-7911-3320-7

Access hundreds of AV2 titles with our digital subscription.
Sign up for a FREE trial at www.openlightbox.com/

The digital components of this book are guaranteed to stay active for at least five years from the date of publication.

2

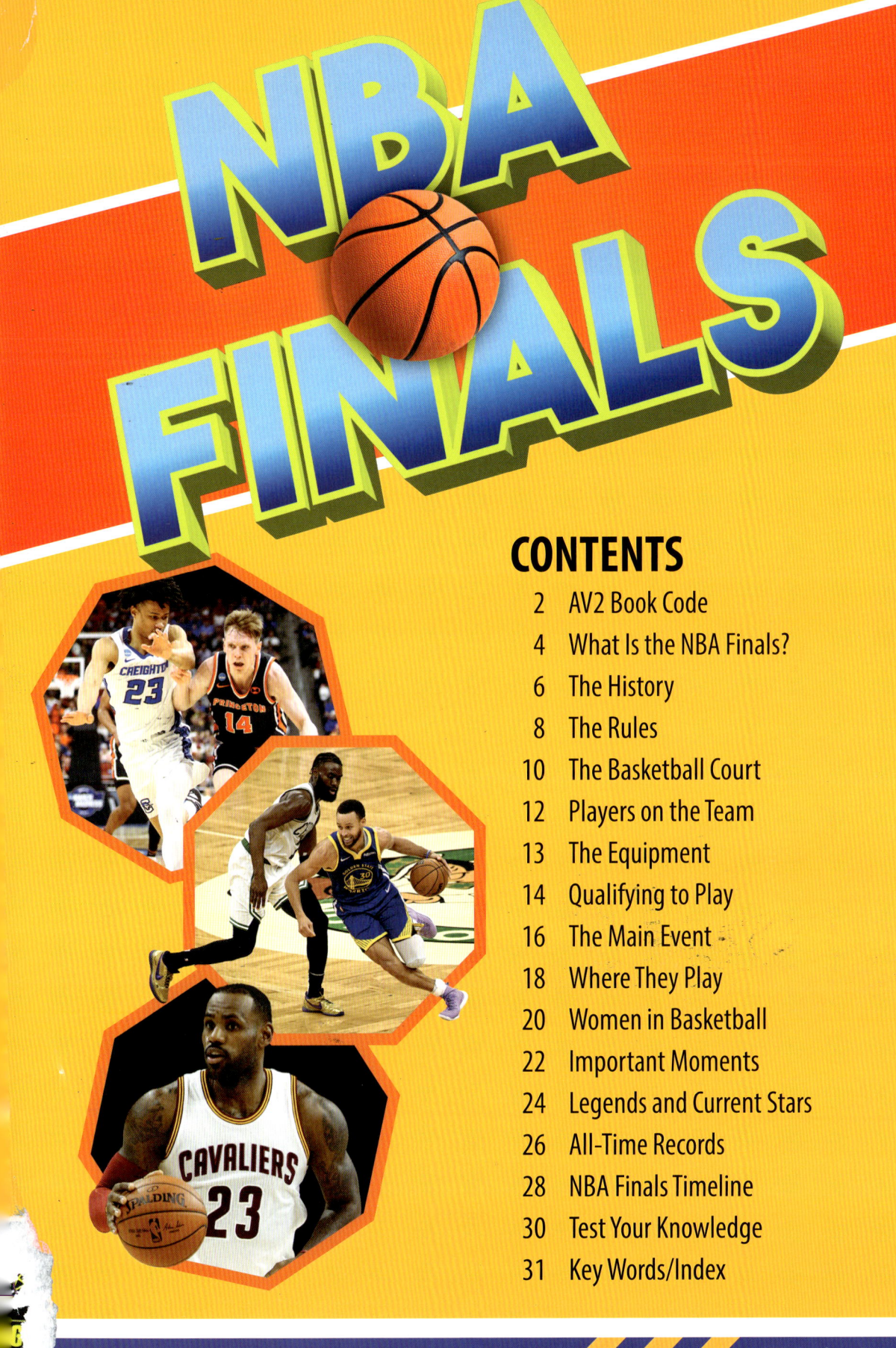

NBA FINALS

CONTENTS

- 2 AV2 Book Code
- 4 What Is the NBA Finals?
- 6 The History
- 8 The Rules
- 10 The Basketball Court
- 12 Players on the Team
- 13 The Equipment
- 14 Qualifying to Play
- 16 The Main Event
- 18 Where They Play
- 20 Women in Basketball
- 22 Important Moments
- 24 Legends and Current Stars
- 26 All-Time Records
- 28 NBA Finals Timeline
- 30 Test Your Knowledge
- 31 Key Words/Index

The Denver Nuggets won the 2023 NBA Finals by defeating the Miami Heat four games to one.

4   Championships

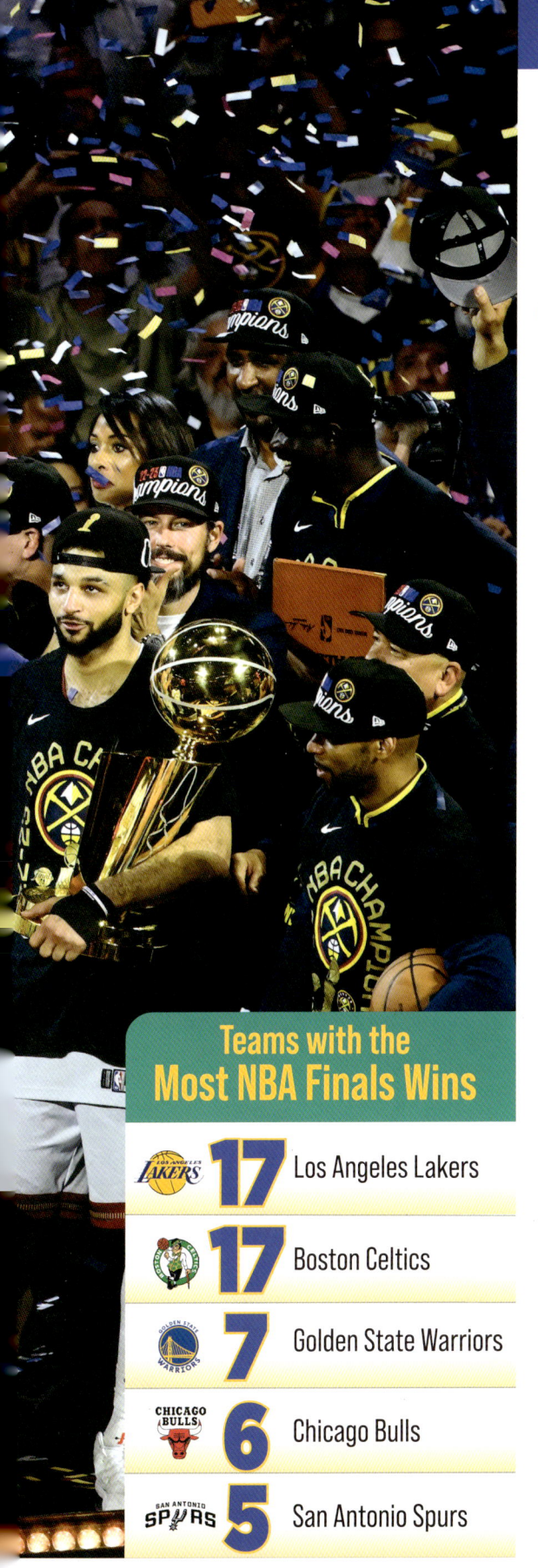

What Is the NBA Finals?

The National Basketball Association (NBA) has 30 teams in the United States and Canada. At the end of the regular season, the top 16 teams **qualify** for the NBA **playoffs**. The NBA Finals is played between the winners of the Eastern **Conference** Finals and the Western Conference Finals.

There have been many unforgettable moments in the NBA and its championship games. Many changed the course of the game or took place as the last seconds ran off the clock. These thrilling moments have made the NBA the world's best-known **professional** basketball league. The NBA Finals are one of the most exciting sports championships.

Teams with the Most NBA Finals Wins

Team	Wins
Los Angeles Lakers	17
Boston Celtics	17
Golden State Warriors	7
Chicago Bulls	6
San Antonio Spurs	5

NBA Finals 5

The History

The NBA was originally known as the Basketball Association of America (BAA). It was formed in 1946. The first BAA championship final was played after the end of the 1946–47 regular season.

In 1949, the BAA merged with the National Basketball League (NBL) to form the NBA. The first official NBA Finals was played in the spring of 1950. The Minneapolis Lakers defeated the Syracuse Nationals in six games.

The Minneapolis Lakers later moved to Los Angeles. They became the Los Angeles Lakers. The Los Angeles Lakers **franchise** and the Boston Celtics are the two most successful teams in NBA history. They have both won the championship 17 times.

Basketball legend George Mikan was part of the Minneapolis Lakers team that won the first NBA championship.

Championships

Game 7 of the 1970 NBA Finals, between the New York Knicks and the Los Angeles Lakers, was named the greatest game in NBA Finals history. The Knicks won the trophy.

Larry O'Brien Championship Trophy

The NBA's championship trophy, known as the Larry O'Brien Championship Trophy, weighs nearly 16 pounds (7.3 kilograms). It is made of silver and bronze and is covered with a thin layer of gold. The trophy stands almost 2 feet (0.6 meters) tall and looks like a large basketball hanging just above a net. The winning NBA team keeps the trophy permanently.

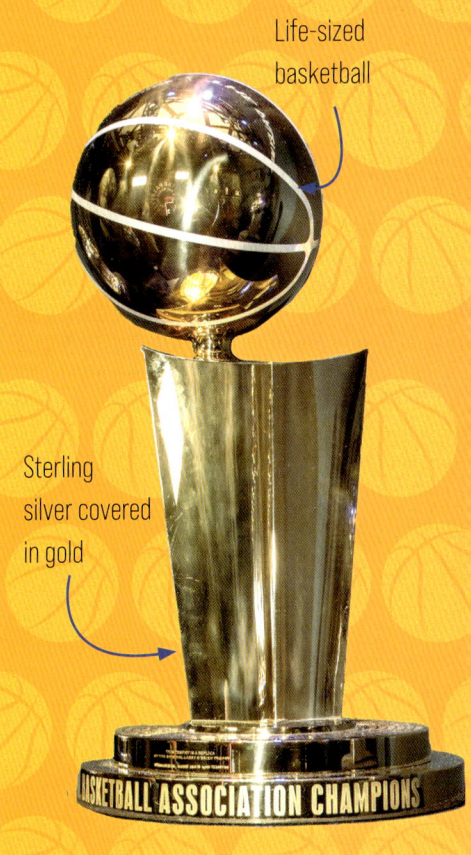

Life-sized basketball

Sterling silver covered in gold

Michael Jordan, one of the best-known basketball players of all time, won six NBA championships with the Chicago Bulls, in 1991, 1992, 1993, 1996, 1997, and 1998.

NBA Finals 7

The Rules

Each basketball team tries to score as many points as possible by putting the ball in the other team's basket. At the end of the game, the team with the most points wins.

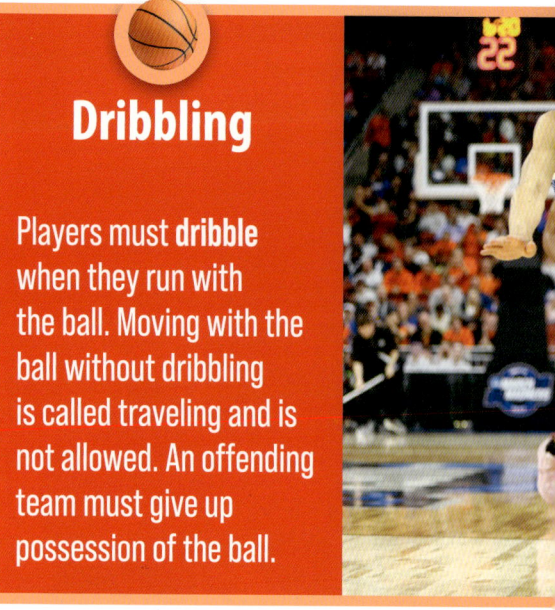

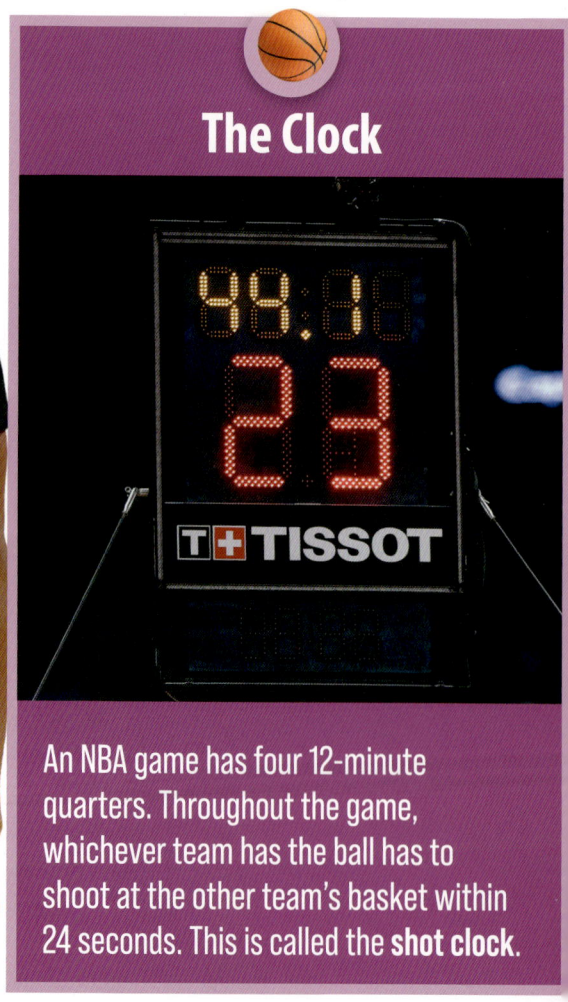

Dribbling

Players must **dribble** when they run with the ball. Moving with the ball without dribbling is called traveling and is not allowed. An offending team must give up possession of the ball.

NBA games are run by a crew chief, two referees, a scorekeeper, two timekeepers, and a replay center official.

The Clock

An NBA game has four 12-minute quarters. Throughout the game, whichever team has the ball has to shoot at the other team's basket within 24 seconds. This is called the **shot clock**.

8 | Championships

Five Players

A team must have five players on the court at all times. Each team has seven extra players, or substitutes. Teams can switch one player with another after any stoppage in play.

Fouls

Players who commit six personal **fouls** must leave the game. A foul on a player who is shooting is punished by a **free throw**. Free throws are worth one point.

NBA Finals 9

The Basketball Court

6 FEET (1.8 m)

16 FEET (4.9 m)

15 FEET (4.6 m)

BASELINE

BACKCOURT

SIDELINE

NBA games are played on a rectangular court 50 feet (15.2 meters) wide and 94 feet (28.7 m) long. Most courts are made of highly polished wood. At each end of the court is a backboard with a basket, or hoop, 10 feet (3 m) above the ground. The court is divided by the midcourt line. The baseline at each end of the court marks the out-of-bounds area.

The lane, or the key, is the colored area in front of the basket. The free-throw line at the top of the key is where foul shots are taken. The three-point line is between 22 feet (6.7 m) and 24 feet (7.3 m) away from the backboard. A scoring shot from inside the three-point line is worth two points. Shots from outside the line are worth three points.

Arena Records

MOST SEATS!
United Center, in Chicago, Illinois, holds **20,917 people** and is the **largest NBA arena**.

OLDEST!
Madison Square Garden, in New York, New York, opened in ... home to the oldest NBA arena.

NEWEST!
Chase Center, in San Francisco, California, opened in **2019** and houses the **newest NBA arena**.

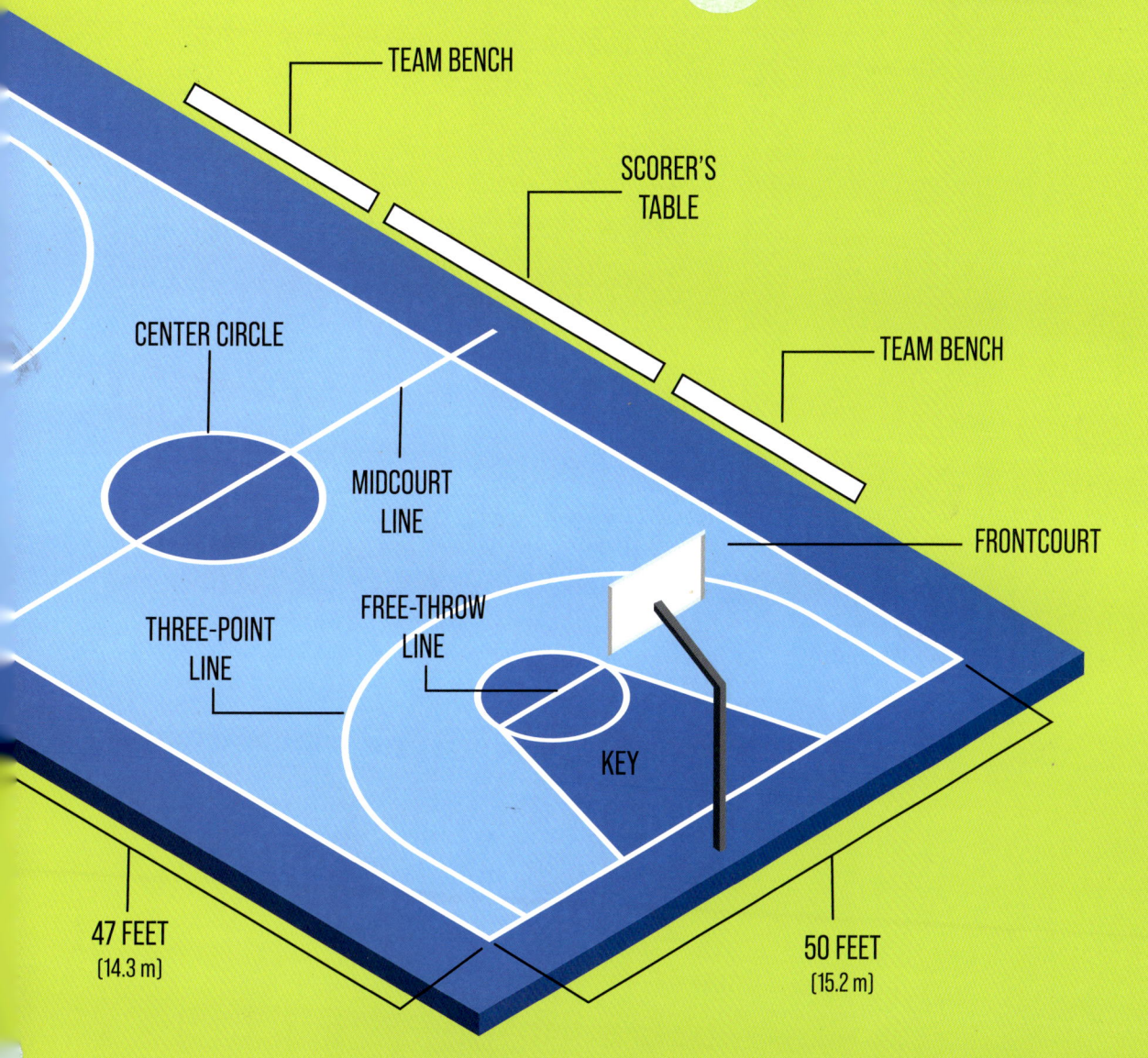

- TEAM BENCH
- SCORER'S TABLE
- TEAM BENCH
- CENTER CIRCLE
- MIDCOURT LINE
- FRONTCOURT
- THREE-POINT LINE
- FREE-THROW LINE
- KEY

47 FEET (14.3 m)

50 FEET (15.2 m)

NBA Finals 11

Players on the Team

There are five positions on a basketball team. Two guards, two forwards, and a center usually play at any one time.

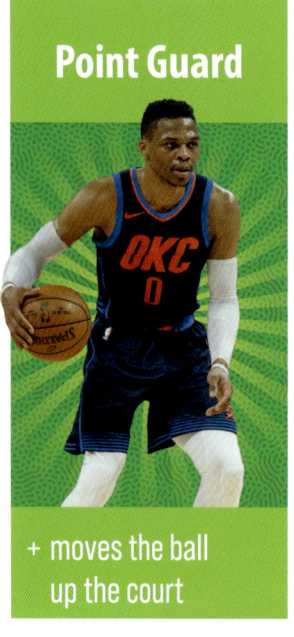

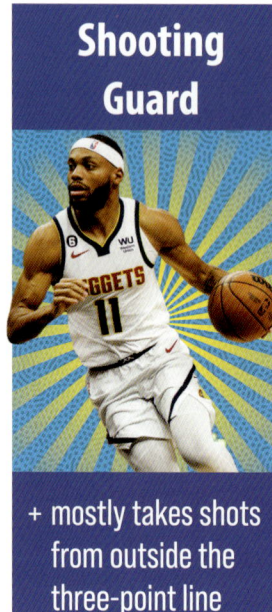

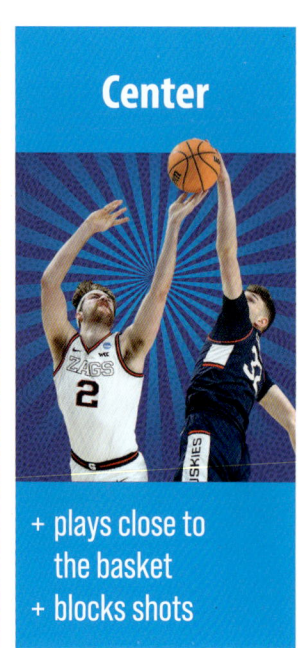

Point Guard
+ moves the ball up the court

Shooting Guard
+ mostly takes shots from outside the three-point line

Small Forward
+ takes both short-range and long-range shots

Power Forward
+ **rebounds** the ball
+ scores on close-range shots

Center
+ plays close to the basket
+ blocks shots

The Equipment

Basketball uniforms are very simple. Players wear a team jersey, team shorts, and athletic shoes.

1 Jersey
Players must tuck their jersey into their shorts. Player numbers are on the front and back of the jersey.

2 Shorts
NBA shorts are usually long and baggy. They are often heavier than other athletic shorts.

3 Shoes
Lightweight basketball shoes have grips to stop players from slipping. The inside of the shoe is cushioned to protect the players' feet when they jump.

NBA Finals 13

Qualifying to Play

There are two conferences in the NBA. Eight teams from each conference make the playoffs. Each round in the conference playoffs is a best-of-seven series. The first team to win four games moves on to the next round.

The team in each conference with the best regular-season record becomes the first seed. That means that four games will be played in that team's home arena if the series goes to seven games.

The NBA playoffs usually start in April and end in June.

James Harden shot a game-winning three-point basket for the Philadelphia 76ers against the Boston Celtics in Round 2 of the 2023 Eastern Conference playoffs.

The Denver Nuggets defeated the Los Angeles Lakers four games to three in the 2023 Western Conference Finals.

14 **Championships**

Nikola Jokić of the Denver Nuggets won the Bill Russell NBA Finals Most Valuable Player (MVP) trophy in the 2023 NBA Finals.

Playoff Brackets

The four teams who win the opening round in each conference move on to the conference semifinals. The winners of that series then meet in the conference finals. The Western Conference champion and the Eastern Conference champion play each other in the NBA Finals.

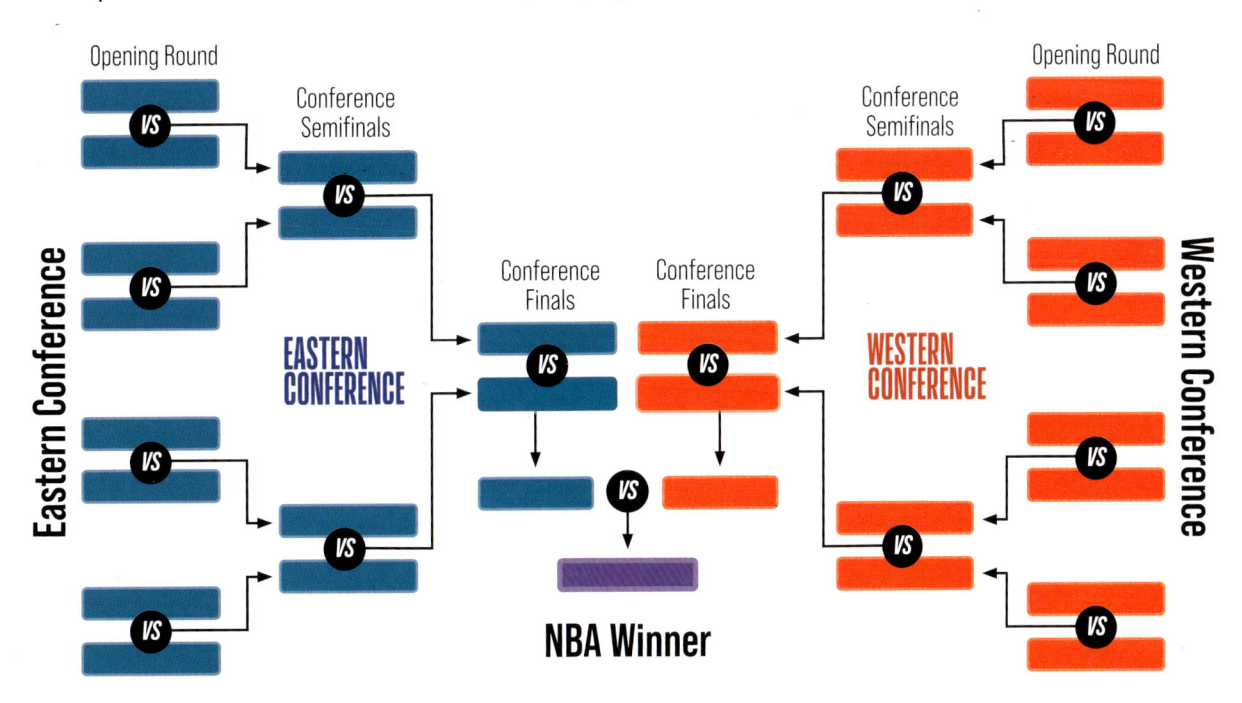

NBA Finals 15

The Main Event

The location of the NBA Finals is decided when the conference champions have been determined. The conference champion with the best regular-season record gets home-court advantage.

The first two games are played in the arena of the team with the best record. The next three games are played on the other team's home court. If they are necessary, the final two games return to the arena where the series started.

2023 NBA Finals

Aaron Gordon scored 27 points for the Nuggets against the Miami Heat in Game 4 of the 2023 NBA Finals.

16 Championships

Inside
The Numbers

2022 NBA Finals

2021 NBA Finals

2020 NBA Finals

Teams with the Most NBA Finals Appearances

LAKERS	**32**	Los Angeles Lakers
CELTICS	**22**	Boston Celtics
WARRIORS	**12**	Golden State Warriors
76ers	**9**	Philadelphia 76ers
KNICKS	**8**	New York Knicks

6 Years of NBA Winners

WINNING TEAM	SERIES RECORD	LOSING TEAM
2023 Denver Nuggets	4-1	2023 Miami Heat
2022 Golden State Warriors	4-2	2022 Boston Celtics
2021 Milwaukee Bucks	4-2	2021 Phoenix Suns
2020 Los Angeles Lakers	4-2	2020 Miami Heat
2019 Toronto Raptors	4-2	2019 Golden State Warriors
2018 Golden State Warriors	4-0	2018 Cleveland Cavaliers

NBA Finals 17

Where They Play

NBA games are played in 27 cities across the United States and in one Canadian city. Each NBA team is based out of an arena. It plays its home games in this arena.

WESTERN CONFERENCE

SOUTHWEST
1. Dallas Mavericks
2. Houston Rockets
3. Memphis Grizzlies
4. New Orleans Pelicans
5. San Antonio Spurs

NORTHWEST
6. Denver Nuggets
7. Minnesota Timberwolves
8. Oklahoma City Thunder
9. Portland Trail Blazers
10. Utah Jazz

PACIFIC
11. Golden State Warriors
12. Los Angeles Clippers
13. Los Angeles Lakers
14. Phoenix Suns
15. Sacramento Kings

EASTERN CONFERENCE

ATLANTIC
16. Boston Celtics
17. Brooklyn Nets
18. New York Knicks
19. Philadelphia 76ers
20. Toronto Raptors

CENTRAL
21. Chicago Bulls
22. Cleveland Cavaliers
23. Detroit Pistons
24. Indiana Pacers
25. Milwaukee Bucks

SOUTHEAST
26. Atlanta Hawks
27. Charlotte Hornets
28. Miami Heat
29. Orlando Magic
30. Washington Wizards

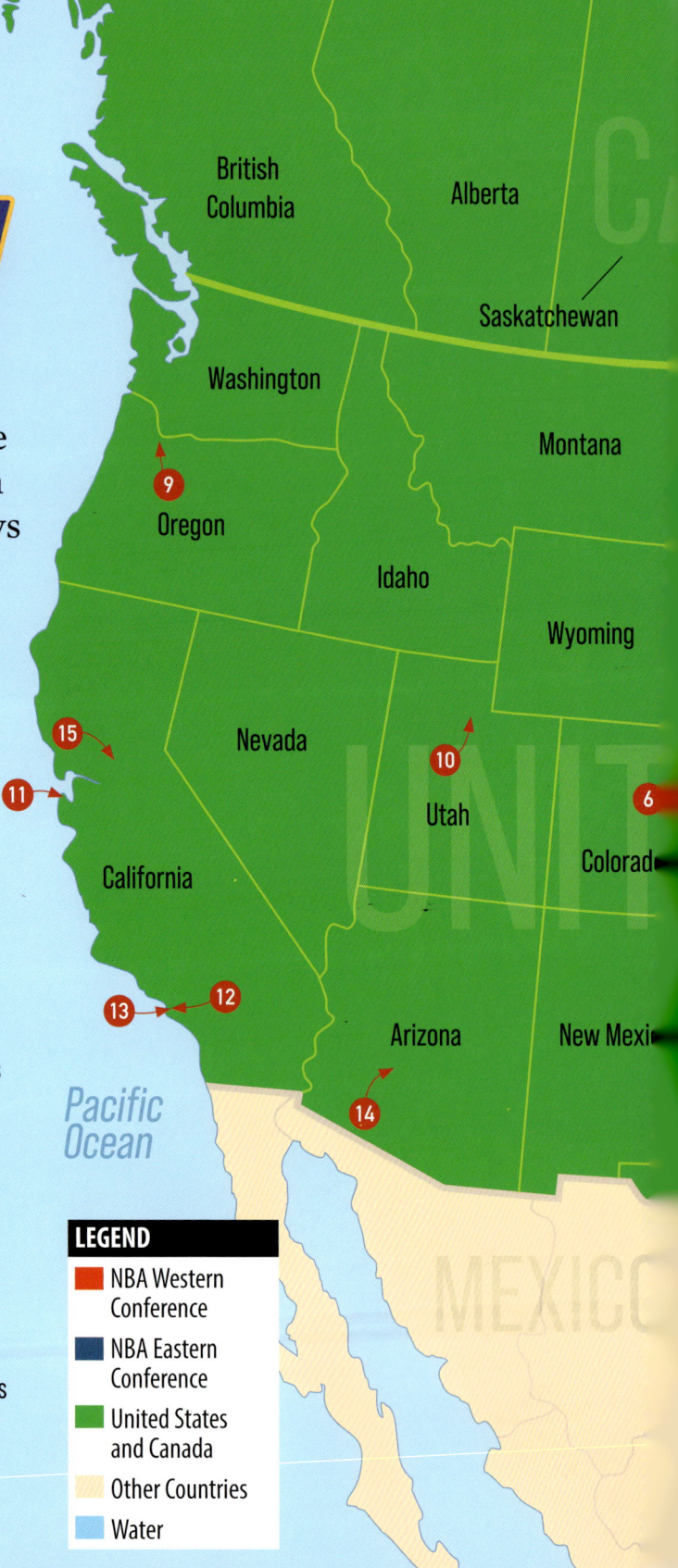

LEGEND
- NBA Western Conference
- NBA Eastern Conference
- United States and Canada
- Other Countries
- Water

18 Championships

NBA Finals 19

Women in Basketball

Sheryl Swoopes
Shooting Guard

The first women's basketball game was played in 1892. Women played on courts divided into three sections. Each section had three players who could not move to another section. Women began playing **full court** basketball in 1971. Five years later, women's basketball was first played at the Olympic Games.

Since 1996, the Women's National Basketball Association (WNBA) has been the best-known professional women's league in the United States. Like the NBA, the WNBA uses a 24-second shot clock. Unlike the NBA, it uses an orange and white ball.

Sheryl Swoopes was the first player signed to play in the WNBA.

9
A'ja Wilson
Power Forward

10
Kelsey Plum
Point Guard

30
Breanna Stewart
Power Forward

NBA Finals 21

Important Moments

George Mikan was one of professional basketball's first star players. He won five championships with the Minneapolis Lakers. In the 1949 championship series, he played two games with a broken wrist.

Elgin Baylor of the Los Angeles Lakers scored an NBA-Finals-record 61 points in a game. He set this record against the Boston Celtics in Game 5 of the 1962 Finals. Baylor's record still stands.

George Mikan was sometimes called "Mr. Basketball."

Elgin Baylor played in the NBA for 14 seasons. In 1996, he was named one of the 50 Greatest Players in NBA History.

In 1980, the Los Angeles Lakers needed to beat the Philadelphia 76ers to win the NBA championship. With star center Kareem Abdul-Jabbar injured, rookie point guard Earvin "Magic" Johnson stepped in to play center in the final game. Johnson scored more than 30 percent of the team's points, and the Lakers won the game 123–107.

"Magic" Johnson led the Los Angeles Lakers to five NBA championships in the 1980s.

In the 2018 NBA Finals, the Golden State Warriors played the Cleveland Cavaliers. This was the fourth straight year they met in the Finals. It marked the first time in U.S. major league sports that the same two teams have met to decide the championship four times in a row.

NBA Finals Record-Holders

8 — Most Consecutive NBA Finals Won
Boston Celtics
1959–1966

6 — Most NBA Finals MVP Awards
Michael Jordan
1991–1998

20 YEARS OLD — Youngest NBA Finals MVP
"Magic" Johnson
1980

21 — Most Assists in a Finals Game
"Magic" Johnson
1984

11 — Most NBA Championships
Bill Russell
1957–1969

NBA Finals 23

Legends and Current Stars

Kareem Abdul-Jabbar
Center

Kareem Abdul-Jabbar was drafted by the Milwaukee Bucks in 1969 and won his first NBA championship in 1971. In 1975, Abdul-Jabbar was traded to the Los Angeles Lakers. Playing center, he helped the team win five NBA titles. During his career, Abdul-Jabbar won six MVP awards and scored more points than any other player in NBA history.

Michael Jordan
Shooting Guard/Small Forward

Michael Jordan is often called the best basketball player of all time. He won six NBA championships as a shooting guard for the Chicago Bulls and was named the NBA Finals MVP six times. Jordan could shoot, move the ball upcourt, pass, block shots, and rebound. He earned the nickname "Air Jordan" because he could leap higher than most other players.

All-Time Rankings

Michael Jordan
RANKED #1
Years Active: 1984–1998, 2001–2003

LeBron James
RANKED #2
Years Active: 2003–Present

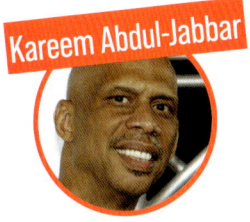

Kareem Abdul-Jabbar
RANKED #3
Years Active: 1969–1989

LeBron James
Small Forward/Power Forward

LeBron James won Rookie of the Year in his first NBA season. He became the youngest player to reach several career benchmarks, including scoring 10,000 career points. He has played for the Cleveland Cavaliers, Miami Heat, and Los Angeles Lakers. James won two Finals with the Heat, and one each with the Cavaliers and the Lakers. He has been named Finals MVP four times.

Nikola Jokić
Center

Center Nikola Jokić was born in Serbia. He is a five-time NBA **All-Star** and won the regular-season NBA MVP award in 2021 and 2022. In 2023, he led the Denver Nuggets to their first NBA championship and won the NBA Finals MVP. Jokić is famous for his unusual passes, which help set up his teammates to score.

NBA Finals

All-Time Records

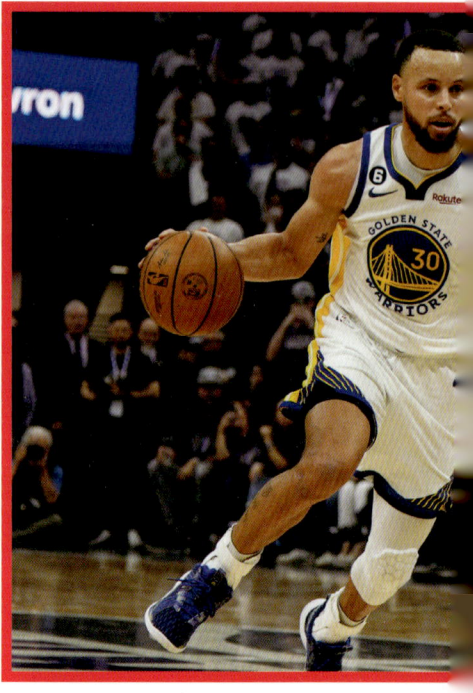

15,837

Kareem Abdul-Jabbar holds the record for most field goals made.

1,192

AC Green of the Los Angeles Lakers holds the record for most consecutive games played.

26 Championships

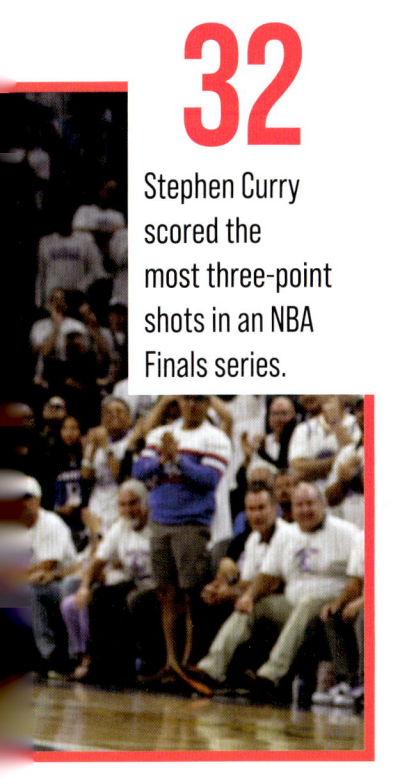

32
Stephen Curry scored the most three-point shots in an NBA Finals series.

23,924
Wilt Chamberlain holds the record for the most rebounds in NBA history.

15,806
John Stockton has made more career assists than any other player.

NBA Finals

NBA Finals Timeline

The NBA Finals has a history of awe-inspiring and surprising moments. Many legendary players and teams have left their mark.

1957 — The Boston Celtics win their first NBA Finals. They go on to win 16 more championships between 1958 and 2016.

1968 — The Boston Celtics win the NBA Finals with Bill Russell acting as both their All-Star center and head coach. He is the first African American coach in the league.

28 Championships

1976 Game 5 of the NBA Finals, between the Boston Celtics and Phoenix Suns, is called the greatest NBA game ever played. The Celtics just barely win in the Finals' first triple overtime, and go on to win the championship in Game 6.

2020 The NBA Finals are played in a bubble at Walt Disney World, in Orlando, Florida, to protect players from the COVID-19 pandemic.

2010 The Los Angeles Lakers beat the Boston Celtics in the NBA Finals. This is the Lakers' 31st NBA Finals appearance, the most of any team in NBA history.

2023 Up to 1 million fans greet the Nuggets in downtown Denver after they win the championship in their first NBA Finals appearance.

NBA Finals 29

TEST YOUR KNOWLEDGE

- 1 -
Which two teams have **won** the **most** NBA Finals?

- 2 -
How many **teams** are in the NBA?

- 3 -
In what **year** was the NBA created?

- 4 -
What are the **dimensions** of an official NBA **court**?

- 5 -
Which of the two teams playing in the NBA Finals gets **home-court** advantage?

- 6 -
What is the **name** of the best-known professional **women's** basketball league in the United States?

- 7 -
How many **teams** from each conference go to the **playoffs**?

- 8 -
What is the name of the **trophy** that the NBA champions receive?

- 9 -
How many seconds are on the NBA **shot clock**?

- 10 -
Who was the first **African American coach** in the NBA?

ANSWERS: **1** The Boston Celtics and Los Angeles Lakers **2** 30 **3** 1949 **4** 50 feet (15.2 m) wide and 94 feet (28.7 m) long **5** The team with the best regular-season record **6** Women's National Basketball Association (WNBA) **7** Eight teams **8** The Larry O'Brien Championship Trophy **9** 24 **10** Bill Russell

30 **Championships**

Key Words

All-Star: an outstanding player selected to represent the Western or Eastern Conference in an annual exhibition game

conference: an association of sports teams within a league that regularly play each other

dribble: to continuously bounce a basketball to move it up the court

fouls: unfair actions that stop an opponent from scoring or moving the ball

franchise: a team or organization that can be associated with a particular location

free throw: a shot at the basket awarded because of a foul on a player

full court: playing on the entire basketball court

playoffs: games played after the end of the regular season

professional: an athlete who is paid to play sports

qualify: to be eligible for a round of competition by reaching a certain standard

rebounds: takes possession of the ball after a missed shot

shot clock: a clock that indicates how much time a team has to shoot the ball at the basket

Index

Abdul-Jabbar, Kareem 23, 24, 25, 26
arena 11, 14, 16, 18

Basketball Association of America (BAA) 6
Boston Celtics 5, 6, 14, 17, 18, 22, 23, 28, 29, 30

court 9, 10, 12, 16, 20, 30

Denver Nuggets 4, 14, 15, 16, 17, 18, 25, 29,

Eastern Conference 5, 14, 15, 18

fouls 9, 10

James, LeBron 25
Johnson, Earvin "Magic" 23
Jokić, Nikola 15, 25
Jordan, Michael 7, 23, 24, 25

Larry O'Brien Championship Trophy 7, 30
Los Angeles Lakers 5, 6, 7, 14, 17, 18, 22, 23, 24, 25, 26, 29, 30

Mikan, George 6, 22

playoffs 5, 14, 15, 30
positions 12

shot clock 8, 20, 30

uniforms 13

Western Conference 5, 14, 15, 18
Women's National Basketball Association (WNBA) 20, 30

NBA Finals 31

Get the best of both worlds.

AV2 bridges the gap between print and digital.

The expandable resources toolbar enables quick access to content including **videos**, **audio**, **activities**, **weblinks**, **slideshows**, **quizzes**, and **key words**.

Animated videos make static images come alive.

Resource icons on each page help readers to further **explore key concepts**.

Published by Lightbox Learning Inc.
276 5th Avenue, Suite 704 #917
New York, NY 10001
Website: www.openlightbox.com

Copyright ©2024 Lightbox Learning Inc.
All rights reserved. No part of this publication may be reproduced, stored in a retrieval system, or transmitted in any form or by any means, electronic, mechanical, photocopying, recording, or otherwise, without the prior written permission of the publisher.

Library of Congress Control Number: 2023941804

ISBN 978-1-7911-5802-6 (hardcover)
ISBN 978-1-7911-5804-0 (softcover)
ISBN 978-1-7911-7804-8 (multi-user eBook)

Printed in Guangzhou, China
1 2 3 4 5 6 7 8 9 0 27 26 25 24 23 23

112023
101322

Project Coordinator Priyanka Das
Art Director Terry Paulhus

Photo Credits
Every reasonable effort has been made to trace ownership and to obtain permission to reprint copyright material. The publisher would be pleased to have any errors or omissions brought to its attention so that they may be corrected in subsequent printings. The publisher acknowledges Alamy, Dreamstime, Getty Images, Newscom, Shutterstock, and Wikimedia as its primary image suppliers for this title.

View new titles and product videos at www.openlightbox.com